Scholastic's
The Magic School Bus

PLANTS SEEDS
A Book About How Living Things Grow

SCHOLASTIC INC.
New York   Toronto   London   Auckland   Sydney

211 4405

Based on the episode from the animated TV series produced by Scholastic Productions, Inc. Based on *The Magic School Bus* book series written by Joanna Cole and illustrated by Bruce Degen.

TV tie-in book adaptation by Patricia Relf and illustrated by John Speirs.
TV script written by Ronnie Krauss, Brian Meehl, and Jocelyn Stevenson.

Library of Congress Cataloging-in-Publication Data available.

ISBN 0-590-22296-1

36 35 34 33 32 31 30 29 28 27 26   04 03 02

Printed in the U.S.A.   24

First Scholastic printing, February 1995

Every class probably learns about plants and seeds.
But not every class has Ms. Frizzle for a teacher.

When Ms. Frizzle does something, she goes all the way. She started by letting us plant a whole garden behind our school.

A photographer was coming
to take a picture of our garden,
so we all wanted it to look its best.

These tomatoes will win prizes!

"To think that these beautiful tomato plants started from tiny seeds," Carlos said. "Add some soil, sunshine, water, and some tender, loving care, and you've got this great garden."

"And once that photographer takes our picture, we'll be famous!" Carlos said. "We could be on the cover of *Plant It!* magazine! Would you like me to autograph your seed packet, Dorothy Ann?"

"I'll think about it!" said Dorothy Ann.

Phoebe was not as excited as Carlos. "I wish I had the beautiful plant I raised at my old school."

Tim put the finishing touch on a drawing.

Phoebe smiled. "That's it! Thank you, Tim," she said. "Still, I wish I had the real thing for our picture this afternoon."

Ms. Frizzle spotted the drawing. "Your plant looks lovely, Phoebe," she said. "Not to worry! It's a simple matter to stop by your old school on a little field trip!"

We all piled onto the old school bus. Carlos was worried that we might not get back in time for the photographer. "This could take all day! Couldn't we fly or something, Ms. Frizzle?"

"Excellent idea, Carlos!" she said. Suddenly the whole bus began to spin. It rose in the air as if it had wings. It did have wings! We were riding in a ladybug!

As we flew over buildings and trees, Phoebe began to look nervous. "What if Mr. Seedplot sees us?" she asked. "We never turned into ladybugs when *he* was my teacher."

Just then, we all saw a school below. Phoebe stared. "There it is!" she gasped.

The bus swooped in low through the school's garden. It looked like a jungle. "Here's the perfect landing pad—I mean, petal," said Ms. Frizzle. The bus landed with a bounce and crawled along the petal of a huge flower.

This is one of my plants!

We crawled one step too far. Suddenly, our ladybug bus slid into something wet and slippery.

"We're stuck in some goop!" Ralphie yelled.

"It's called nectar," Dorothy Ann said.

"Follow me, class!" said the Friz. She opened the doors and slipped out into the lake of nectar.

We didn't know it then, but Mr. Seedplot could have reached out and picked us. "Phoebe's plants certainly have grown well," he said to himself. "She worked hard on them. I really should take one to her new school for her."

Mr. Seedplot heard a buzz and looked up. "Ah, bees! I won't disturb their work right now," he said, turning to a patch of tomato plants.

We also saw the bees coming . . . and they were headed right into our flower.

"Yikes! Air raid!" shouted Arnold.

"Glory bee!" said the Friz happily. "As soon as these bees drink enough nectar, then we can crawl out of here. All aboard the ladybus, please. Next stop, anther!"

Dorothy Ann is amazing. Even upside down, she could remember what she had read that morning. "The *anther* is the part of the flower that makes pollen," she said.

These yellow balls are pollen? Pollen makes me . . . ah . . . ah . . . CHOO! . . . sneeze.

There we were, on top of the anther, with bees buzzing all around us.

It was then that Phoebe caught sight of her old teacher. "It's Mr. Seedplot!" she yelled. "He'll see us! Do something! Fast!"

Ms. Frizzle stayed calm. "No problem," she said cheerfully. "We'll get out of here the same way the pollen does."

Cool! That bee is covered in pollen!

Uh-oh! Ah-choo!

Ms. Frizzle pressed a yellow button, and we shrank again. Now we were as small as a grain of pollen.

"Whew!" said Phoebe. "That was close!"

Carlos was not so happy. "We'll never get back to school in time for the photographer," he grumbled.

"*Bee* of good cheer. We're on our way," said Ms. Frizzle. "Hang on!" she called as the leg of a passing bee swept us up and away.

Off we flew, stuck to the leg of that bee. It was a short ride. At the very next plant, the bee bumped a flower and brushed us off, along with a lot of pollen.

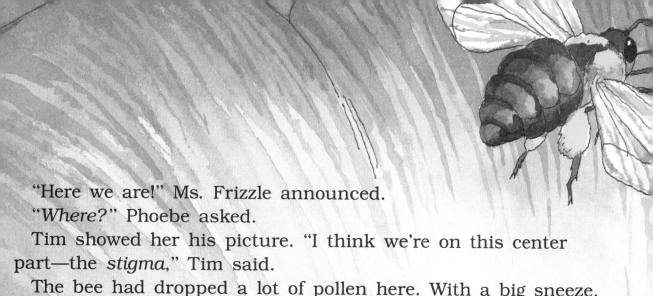

"Here we are!" Ms. Frizzle announced.

"*Where*?" Phoebe asked.

Tim showed her his picture. "I think we're on this center part—the *stigma*," Tim said.

The bee had dropped a lot of pollen here. With a big sneeze, Arnold bumped into a grain of pollen, knocked it over . . . and fell down some kind of tunnel underneath!

Arnold found a pollen tube!

h-choo!

Phoebe looked down the tube. "Mr. Seedplot will never spot us down there!" she said, and she hopped into the tube and slid down.

Ms. Frizzle beamed. "That's the spirit! Take chances! Make mistakes! Check out pollen tubes! Yahoo!" she yelled as she, too, jumped down the tube.

We all slid to the bottom of the pollen tube.

"*Now* where are we?" asked Carlos. "Couldn't we just grab one of Phoebe's plants and go back to school?"

"I don't think we need a whole plant," Keesha said. "Look at this!" She pointed to something that looked like a big rock. "It's a seed!"

"I get it!" Dorothy Ann said. "When pollen from one flower lands on the stigma of another, it grows a pollen tube, finds one of these egg cells, and together they make a seed!"

Carlos still wasn't happy. "No seed can grow into a plant by three o'clock," he said.

"Not without some help," said Ms. Frizzle. She reached into the bus and pressed a button . . . and suddenly things went wild. The seeds were growing bigger and sprouting hair!

"We need to hurry things along a bit," said Ms. Frizzle. "Everyone on the bus, please!"

We all rushed back to the bus, the doors slammed shut, and we drove up and onto one of the biggest seeds.

As the seeds around us grew bigger, the flower burst open. We felt the sun shine in and a breeze blowing through the windows of the bus. Suddenly our seed flew into the air—with us on board.

Those hairs are like a parachute!

Away we flew on the back of our seed, carried along on gusts of wind.

Carlos still worried. "Can't we go any faster?" he asked.

"Well," Ms. Frizzle said, "This is pretty fast for a seed. But there are seeds that travel by attaching themselves to dogs or birds . . . or people," she said, eyeing a man on a bicycle.

"*No!*" croaked Phoebe. "That's Mr. Seedplot!" But she was too late. Our seed had landed in Mr. Seedplot's hair. "Oh, how embarrassing!" Phoebe groaned.

We were almost home, still stuck in Mr. Seedplot's hair, and
we hadn't even been introduced. So we all shouted, "Hello,
Mr. Seedplot!"—except for Phoebe, who was too embarrassed
to talk. But when Mr. Seedplot swung his head to see who
was calling him, we flew off.

"Last stop!" Ms. Frizzle announced. She pushed a button.
Poof! The bus got big again. She pushed another button. *Poof!*
The seed, which had landed in our garden, grew into a tall
plant with beautiful flowers.

"Ah, there you are!" Mr. Seedplot said when he spotted us. "I brought one of Phoebe's plants, but I see that she already has one. Nice to see you again, Ms. Frizzle."

Phoebe gasped. "You mean you've met Ms. Frizzle before?" she said.

Mr. Seedplot smiled. "Yes. She's a very special person."

PLANT IT!

The Magic of Gardening

We had to agree. Ms. Frizzle is special, all right!

Letter to the Editor of *Plant It!* magazine

Dear Editor,

   I liked the pictures of the garden planted by Ms. Frizzle's class. But there are a few things I'd like to point out to you about your article.

   • First of all, I have never heard of a school bus that could turn into a ladybug or a grain of pollen.

   • Second, I don't see how anyone could be allergic to such a big grain of pollen. It could never get inside his nose!

   • Also, I would like to know how anyone could make a seed or plant grow in just a few seconds. Even with my secret homemade fertilizer recipe, my plants take a long time to grow and to make seeds—like days, weeks, or even months!

   • In fact, I don't think I've ever seen a plant quite like Phoebe's. Did you invent that plant?

   • And you must have done some kind of trick photography on Ms. Frizzle's clothes, because *no one* dresses like that.

Your faithful reader,
D. Tractor

Dear Reader,

   You are absolutely right. Could you send us your fertilizer recipe?

—The Editor

A Note to Parents, Teachers, and Kids

A seed is a tiny plant in a wonderfully efficient package, ready to grow when conditions are right. This book tells the story of seeds and the flowers that make them.

- Pollen is manufactured by the anther, the top part of a flower's stamen. This is the male part of the flower.

- The colors, markings, and scents of flowers attract animals such as bees and hummingbirds, which drink the flower's nectar and carry its pollen to other flowers. Pollen may also travel on the wind (as with grasses and many trees) or water (as with waterweed).

- When pollen lands on the stigma of its own kind of flower, it grows a pollen tube that reaches down the pistil to the ovary, the female part of the flower. A sperm cell from the pollen travels down the tube and joins with an egg cell. The fertilized egg cell begins to divide and becomes a seed.

- Seeds travel in many ways: on the wind, by attaching themselves to animals or to people's clothing, in the digestive tracts of animals, or by bursting forcefully from a pod or fruit.

Children can enjoy their own plant adventure by looking for these parts on different kinds of flowers, and by planting seeds themselves.

Ms. Frizzle